The Ultimate 1 Year Old Activity Book

Autumn McKay

D1557790

Find me on Instagram!
@BestMomIdeas

The Ultimate 1 Year Old Activity Book by Autumn McKay
Published by Creative Ideas Publishing

www.BestMomIdeas.com

For permissions contact:
Permissions@BestMomIdeas.com

ISBN: 978-1-952016-43-1

Table of Contents

Ⓢ *Sensory*   Ⓖ *Gross Motor Skills*   Ⓒ *Crafts*

Ⓕ *Fine Motor Skills*   Ⓞ *Outdoor*   Ⓘ *Independent*

⭐ *Low Prep*

Table of Contents

S *Sensory*   G *Gross Motor Skills*   C *Crafts*

F *Fine Motor Skills*   O *Outdoor*   I *Independent*

☆ *Low Prep*

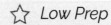

Table of Contents

Ⓢ *Sensory*   Ⓖ *Gross Motor Skills*   Ⓒ *Crafts*

Ⓕ *Fine Motor Skills*   Ⓞ *Outdoor*   Ⓘ *Independent*

☆ *Low Prep*

Table of Contents

(S) *Sensory*　　(G) *Gross Motor Skills*　　(C) *Crafts*

(F) *Fine Motor Skills*　　(O) *Outdoor*　　(I) *Independent*

☆ *Low Prep*

About Me

My name is Autumn. I am a wife to an incredible husband, and a mother to two precious boys and a sweet little girl!

I have a Bachelor's of Science degree in Early Childhood Education. I have taught in the classroom and as an online teacher. I have earned teacher certifications in Arizona, Colorado, California, and Georgia. However, one of my greatest joys is being a mom! After my first son was born, I wanted to be involved in helping him learn and grow so I began to

develop color lessons to help engage his developing mind. I also wanted to help other moms dealing with hectic schedules and continuous time restraints. These activities evolved into my first book, called **Toddler Lesson Plans: Learning Colors**.

My children and I continue to enjoy doing activities together, but my newest niece and nephew have inspired me to write an activity book for those that aren't quite ready to learn colors or do the activities from **The Ultimate Toddler Activity Guide**. The book you hold in your hands, **The Ultimate 1 Year Old Activity Book**, is full of activities that I know your 1 year old will enjoy. Many 1-year old children explore the world through their senses, so many of these activities are sensory based. Through my learning time with my children I have created theses additional books:

Toddler Lesson Plans: Learning ABC's

The Ultimate Toddler Activity Guide

The Ultimate Preschool Activity Guide

The Ultimate Kindergarten Prep Guide

Learning Numbers Workbook

Learning Preschool Math Workbook

Learning Kindergarten Math Workbook

Learning 1st Grade Math Workbook

Learning ABC's Workbook: Print

Learning ABC's Workbook: Precursive

I hope that your little ones can benefit from these activities just like my children, nieces, and nephews! I have also developed a website called BestMomIdeas.com. It's a place where moms are encouraged to be the best version of themselves by feeling understood and never judged.

Benefits of Activity Time

Did you know that 90% of a child's brain develops by age 5? This means that almost all of a child's brain is developed before they reach kindergarten! So, take advantage of your child's brain development in the early years by beginning an activity time!

"Activity time" refers to activating or stimulating a child's body and/or brain. This typically involves a hands-on experience for the toddler where he is engaged in reading, running, climbing, coloring, pouring, etc.

Let me explain how the brain develops. When a baby is born, he* is born with all the neurons (brain cells) that he will have for the rest of his life. Although most of the brain's neurons are present at birth, the neurons are not mature. Neurons have branches called dendrites and axons that transfer information from neuron to neuron. These branches on the neurons are crucial in brain development. The number of branches increases dramatically as a child is exposed to things around him. If the connections are used regularly, then they stay. But if the connections aren't used, they are pruned and die off. The more stimulation or exposure to experiences a child has, the thicker the connections become. It's much harder for these connections to be formed later in life.

Loving interactions with parents or caregivers help prepare a brain for learning. Every time you play, read, cook, garden, color, or do an educational activity with your child, these activities are building connections in your child's developing brain.

*As you begin your journey through this book, I need to mention that in most of the activities I address your child with the pronoun "he." I did this for simplicity and ease of writing, however, please know, as I wrote this book I was thinking of your precious little girl as well.

Additional Helpful Hints

Everything is new and mysterious to young toddlers. A toddler wants to explore and soak in the exciting world that surrounds him, but is he ready to be doing educational activities at this age? The short answer is yes. Children at this age learn through their senses. They learn through feeling, smelling, seeing, hearing, and even tasting. That is why this book contains mostly sensory, play-based activities. Furthermore, there are activities that allow your toddler to develop his gross (big muscles) and fine (finger muscles) skills, create and work independently.

I chose to organize this book in alphabetical order; however, beside each activity in the *Table of Contents* and throughout the book I have denoted what developmental objective your child will achieve by completing the activities. Here is a key:

S **Sensory:** These will be activities that allow your child to learn through his senses. Sensory experiences help children develop cognitive and motor skills, language, creativity, and problem-solving skills. He might use his sense of sight to be introduced to colors or his sense of touch to feel different textures.

F **Fine Motor Skills**: These activities will allow your toddler to practice using the muscles in his fingers. The activities help make the hand and finger muscles stronger so that one day he will be able to hold a pencil and write.

G **Gross Motor Skills**: These activities will allow your child to develop the big muscles in his body. The activities let him work on balance, coordination, and strength.

O **Outdoor:** These activities I recommend doing outdoors for easier cleanup.

C **Crafts**: These activities are fun crafts that your toddler can enjoy.

I **Independent**: These activities can be done by your toddler independently. You are welcome to do them with your child, but if you have dinner to prepare, a phone call to make, or laundry to do then these are the perfect activities to keep your toddler busy for a few minutes.

I know many parents are very busy and do not have a lot of time to set up an activity so I have placed a "star" beside all activities that should only take a minute or two to prep. I hope these low/no prep activities make life just a little easier for you, especially on busy days.

 *Low Prep*

To help you prepare your materials in advance, look ahead and pick out a couple activities you want to do with your toddler. At this time make a list of all the materials you will need to buy during your next shopping trip to the grocery store.

To help make life a little easier for you, you can access a comprehensive materials list for all activities through this link:

www.bestmomideas.com/1-year-old-printouts

Password: bestmomideas26y8

A Gift For You

In appreciation of your purchase of this book, I would like to provide you with a link to enjoy 4 free activities your child is sure to enjoy. These activities are from **Toddler Lesson Plans: Learning Colors** and **The Ultimate Toddler Activity Guide**. Please follow the link below to access your free activities.

www.bestmomideas.com/1-year-old-printouts

Password: bestmomideas26y8

Play Your Way to Learning

Nothing is more charming than a child's face and the many expressions of joy a child exhibits in play and learning. Learning can be so fun! Playtime can be an enjoyable moment for the entire family. Throughout these pages, you will find many wonderful activities which hold the potential to bring a smile to your child's face and joy in your home. My hope is that in the midst of your children "playing their way" to growth and knowledge, this book will help flood your home with joy.

I want to reiterate that the goal of this book is to provide activities that you can enjoy with your child. The activities in this book are written for a young toddler. However, these years are a time of many developmental milestones. Each child is unique and matures at his or her own pace. If you sense your child is becoming frustrated with an activity, please be sensitive and do not push your child to continue. Without question, you know your child best and what he is capable of attempting. If you feel an activity is beyond your child's present ability, simply move to another activity. There are many great "child tested" activities from which to choose.

Remember, even though significant learning will occur as you engage your child in these activities, I want you and your child to have fun! Often when my children pray, they each end their prayer with the statement, "...And let us have a fun day, Amen." In the midst of hectic days and the constant pressure to perform, a child deserves a fun day. The truth is you deserve a "fun day" as well. It is my desire that in the following pages you will discover a path for your toddler to learn, and an avenue through which you will experience immense satisfaction as YOU have a fun day and enjoy your child.

I hope these activities bring as much joy and learning to your home as they have mine!

Activities

☆ Animal Exercise

> **Developmental Objective:** This outside activity allows your child to develop his gross motor skills by making big movements as he pretends to move like an animal.

Directions:

> **Quick Tip:** This activity can be done indoors or outdoors. It might be nice to have a change of scenery and do the activity outdoors if the weather allows.

1. Young toddlers enjoy learning about animals and the sounds animals make, but this fun activity teaches children how animals move while building their balance and big muscle skills. I recommend doing this activity alongside your child. Ask your toddler to be different animals with you.

2. Call out an animal and ask your child to say the sound the animal makes. Complete the animal movement together.

3. Here is a list of ideas:

   a.   Waddle like a duck

   b.   Flap your wings like a bird

   c.   Hop like a frog

   d.   Slither like a snake

   e.   Bounce like a kangaroo

   f.   Stomp like an elephant

   g.   Swim like a fish

   h.   Gallop like a horse

   i.   Wag your tail like a dog

   j.   Crawl like a cat

The Ultimate 1 Year Old Activity Book | Autumn McKay

Animal Tape Rescue

> **Developmental Objective:** This activity helps your toddler build the muscles and
> coordination in his fingers as he unpeels the tape.

Materials:

- ☐ Table
- ☐ Small Plastic Animals
- ☐ Painter's Tape

Directions:

1. To set up the activity, gather several small plastic animal figures. (If you don't have plastic animals, you can use toy cars, wooden blocks, or anything small.)

2. Place the animals on the table.

3. Using pieces of painter's tape, cover and attach the animals to the table.

4. Invite your toddler to rescue the animals by peeling the tape off of the table and animals.

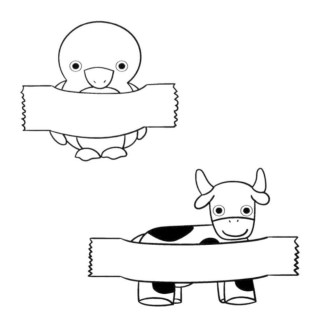

Art in a Bag

> **S** **C** **Developmental Objective:** Your child will create art by using their hands to explore the texture, temperature, and color mixture of the paint.

Materials:

- ☐ Gallon Ziploc Bag
- ☐ 2-3 Washable Paints
- ☐ Cardstock
- ☐ Packing Tape

Directions:

1. To set up the activity, place the cardstock inside the Ziploc bag.

2. You can ask your toddler to pick the paint colors or you can pick the colors yourself.

3. Squirt a dab of each paint color inside the bag.

4. Seal the bag closed.

5. Tape the edges of the bag to a table or solid floor.

6. Invite your child to use his hands or feet (only if the bag is taped to the floor) to move the paint around the bag to create a beautiful piece of art.

7. When he is finished, take the cardstock out of the bag and place in a spot to dry.

☆ Balance Balls

> **G** **I** **Developmental Objective:** This activity allows your child to develop spatial awareness. He will learn how to control the placement of his hand and arm as he places the balls on toilet paper rolls and paper towel rolls. This activity can be completed independently.

Materials:
- ☐ Assortment of Toilet Paper Rolls and Paper Towel Rolls
- ☐ Tennis Balls

Directions:
1. Stand each toilet paper and paper towel roll up on a flat surface.

2. Gather tennis balls.

3. Show your toddler how to place a tennis ball on the top of one toilet paper or paper towel roll.

4. Ask him to place a tennis ball on top of a roll. Encourage him as he works to master this challenge.

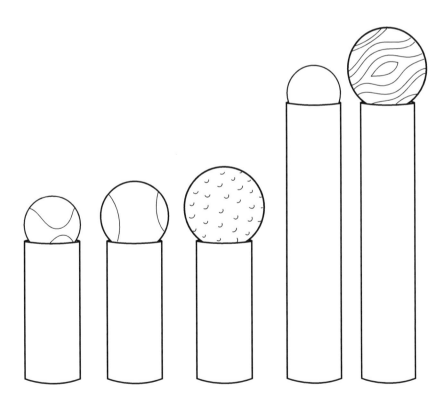

Ball Roll

> **G** **Developmental Objective:** Your toddler will develop his depth perception and spatial awareness as he determines how fast or slow to roll the ball to land it in a cup.

Materials:

- ☐ Tennis Balls
- ☐ 4 Plastic Cups
- ☐ Tape
- ☐ Table

Directions:

1. You can choose to do this activity at a coffee table, side table, or kitchen table.

2. Hold a plastic cup even with the edge of the table you chose.

3. Place a piece of tape from the top of the table to the inside of the cup so that the cup can hang freely from the edge of the table. Tape the remaining three cups to the side of the table.

4. Ask your toddler to stand at the other end of the table—opposite of the cups.

5. Demonstrate how to roll (not throw) the ball across the table and land it in a cup.

6. Now allow him to practice.

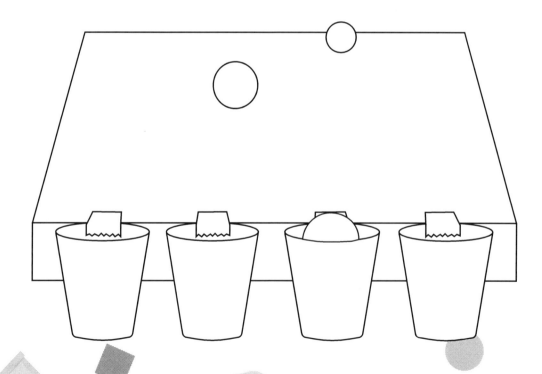

☆ Bean Sensory Bin

> **(S)** **Developmental Objective:** This activity allows your toddler to play tactilely. He can use his hands to explore the texture of beans.

Materials:

- ☐ Large Plastic Container
- ☐ 5lb Bag of Dried Beans
- ☐ Assortment of Toys, Utensils or Cups

Quick Tip: *My children are much older than one years old now and still love playing in a bean sensory bin.*

Directions:

1. Get a large plastic container. (I use a plastic container with a lid so that it is always available when my children want to play.)

2. Pour the 5-pound bag of dried beans (any kind will do) into the container.

3. Add scoops, measuring utensils, toys, or bowls to the beans. Let your child enjoy scooping and pouring the dried beans from one bowl to the next or zooming a tractor through the beans.

Book Drop

> **Developmental Objective:** Your toddler will develop control of his hand, arm, and leg coordination as he bends down to pick up a book and inserts the book into the book drop.

Materials:

- ☐ Large Cardboard Box
- ☐ Scissors
- ☐ Children's Books

Directions:

1. To prepare this activity, get a large cardboard box. Only one side needs to be taped.

2. On the taped side of the box, cut a rectangular slot like a library return box. You will want to cut it to the size of your largest book's edge.

3. Now flip the box over. The flaps do not need to be underneath the box. The box is now similar to a library book return.

4. Stack a variety of books beside the box.

5. Invite your child to pick a book to drop into the slot of the box. You may even offer to read the book, and once you have read the book ask him to drop it in the box.

6. Once he has dropped all books into the box, then you can lift the box to empty the books and start all over again.

MARVELOUS

WINNERS ARE NOT people who NEVER FAIL BUT people who NEVER QUIT

☆ Bowling

G O **Developmental Objective:** This outdoor activity allows your child to strengthen his balancing ability as he stands on one leg to kick a soccer ball.

Materials:

☐ 10 Plastic Cups
☐ Soccer Ball

Quick Tip: This is a fun activity to do outside, but it can be difficult to do outside if it is too windy.

Directions:

1. Stack the 10 plastic cups into a pyramid formation with four cups on the bottom, three cups on the second row, two cups on the third row and one cup on the top. (I like to do it this way because it's more likely the cups will fall over when hit with the ball—making it more enjoyable for the child.)

2. Place your toddler six feet from the pyramid of cups.

3. Ask him to roll or kick the soccer ball towards the pyramid to knock the cups over. It is great to practice both movements of rolling and kicking to work on both big muscle groups.

4. Reset the cups and repeat the game as many times as your child would enjoy.

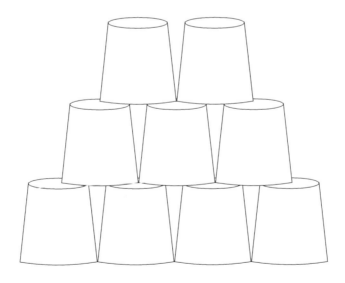

☆ Bubble Sensory Bin

(S)(O) ***Developmental Objective:*** This activity allows your toddler to play tactilely. He can use his hands to explore the texture of bubbles.

Materials:

- ☐ Large Plastic Container
- ☐ Water
- ☐ Food Coloring (Optional)
- ☐ Dish Soap
- ☐ Whisk
- ☐ Water Toys

Directions:

1. In the large plastic container, add ¼ cup of dish soap.

2. Add water and food coloring to the container.

3. Stir together with a whisk.

4. Allow your toddler to play in the bubble bin with various water toys. Explain to him that if he uses the whisk to stir the bubbles it will make more bubbles.

• • • • • • • • • • • • • • •

☆ Build a Tower with Recycling

(G)(I) ***Developmental Objective:*** Your child will become more spatially aware as he learns how to control his hand placement as he stacks the recyclable items. This activity can be completed independently.

Materials:

- ☐ Assortment of Recyclable Items

Directions:

1. Collect items that you would normally throw in a recycling bin. (Ex. egg carton, milk jug, milk carton, boxes, paper towel tubes, etc.)

2. Clean any items that need to be cleaned.

3. Place all items in front of your toddler. Show him how the items can be stacked on or beside each other to form a castle.

4. Ask him to create a tower out of the recyclable items while you complete something you need to do.

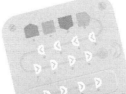

☆ Build with Marshmallows

> **Developmental Objective:** This sensory activity allows your toddler to strengthen the muscles in his hand as he holds a marshmallow.
>
> (S) (F)

Materials:

☐ Regular or Jumbo Size Marshmallows

Quick Tip: It's always a nice treat to taste the marshmallows after construction too.

Directions:

1. It's fun to use different building materials in place of building blocks, so ask your toddler if he would enjoy building a tower out of marshmallows.

2. See how tall he can stack his marshmallows before they fall over.

• • • • • • • • • • • •

Card Slot Drop

> **Developmental Objective:** Your child will develop his pincer grasp as he holds a thin card between his thumb and index finger and slides it into the oatmeal container.
>
> (F)

Materials:

☐ Empty Oatmeal Container with Lid
☐ Deck of Cards
☐ Scissors

Directions:

1. You will need to cut a thin rectangular slot big enough for a card to slide through in the lid of the oatmeal container.

2. Place the lid back on the oatmeal container.

3. Place the container and a deck of cards in front of your child. Show him how to slide a card through the opening of the lid.

4. You may allow your toddler to do this activityindependently, or you can introduce him to the numbers on the cards by counting the figures on the card while you do the activity together.

☆ Cardboard Box Coloring

S **C** **I** **Developmental Objective:** This craft allows your child to explore his visual senses as he chooses different colors to color the cardboard box. This craft can be done independently.

Materials:

☐ Cardboard Box
☐ Crayons

Directions:

1. Place an empty cardboard box on the floor. This activity can be done independently. This activity is also good to be able to keep your todddler in one location.

2. Place an assortment of crayons inside the box.

3. Leave the top of the box open. Now the child can sit in the box and be surrounded by a blank canvas.

4. Ask him to color a picture on each panel inside the box.

• • • • • • • • • • • • •

☆ Catch with a Balloon

G **Developmental Objective:** Your toddler will gain coordination as he moves his arms to catch a balloon.

Materials:

☐ Balloon

Directions:

1. Learning to play catch is a hard skill to master, especially for toddlers, because the ball travels fast, it's hard to grasp the ball, and toddlers aren't very coordinated yet. So, help your toddler learn how to play catch with a balloon.

2. Blow up a balloon and ask your toddler to play catch with you. Balloons travel a lot slower than a ball so it gives your toddler's brain a chance to determine where his hands need to be to catch the balloon.

Quick Tip: Bigger balloons will move slower so size the balloon accordingly. If an older sibling wants to play, give the sibling a slightly smaller balloon for a challenge.

☆ Cereal Transfer

S **O** **F** **Developmental Objective:** This outdoor activity allows your toddler to explore the texture of cereal. Your toddler will strengthen his hand muscles by holding spoons and measuring cups in his hand.

Materials:

- ☐ 2 Large Bowls
- ☐ Cereal
- ☐ Spoons
- ☐ Measuring Cups

Quick Tip: *This activity can get messy so it is best to do it outside.*

Directions:

1. Pour cereal into one large bowl. Leave the other bowl empty.

2. Give your child different kinds of spoons and measuring cups.

3. Ask him to use the spoons and measuring cups to transfer the cereal from the full bowl of cereal to the empty bowl.

• • • • • • • • • • • • • • •

☆ Clothespin Pull

I **F** **Developmental Objective:** Your child will strengthen his pincer grasp as he uses his thumb and index finger to pinch a clothespin.

Materials:

- ☐ Mixing Bowl
- ☐ Clothespins

Directions:

1. Clip clothespins around the rim of the mixing bowl.

2. Show the bowl to your toddler. Ask him to use his index finger and thumb to pinch the top of the clothespin to open and release the clothespin from the bowl.

3. When he completes the activity, you can reset it so he can do it again.

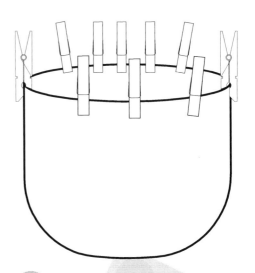

Cloud Dough

 Developmental Objective: This outdoor activity allows your toddler to play tactilely. He can use his hands to explore the texture of cloud dough as he molds it.

Materials:

- ☐ Large Plastic Container
- ☐ 8 Cups Flour
- ☐ 1 Cup Baby Oil
- ☐ Shovels, Cookie Cutters, Cups, etc.

Directions:

1. You can ask your toddler to help you make the cloud dough or you can make it ahead of time. This activity makes for an easier cleanup when played outside.

2. In the plastic container, mix together the flour and the baby oil. It will still look like flour, but it becomes more moldable.

3. Invite your child to play in the cloud dough with you. Ask him to form the dough into balls, build a castle, dig, or bury things.

• • • • • • • • • • • • • •

Color Bin

Developmental Objective: Your toddler will develop his visual senses as he explores items of one color.

Materials:

- ☐ Basket
- ☐ Objects of the Same Color

Directions:

1. Pick a single color and gather objects of that color from around your home. Place the items in a basket.

   a. For example, if you pick red, place an apple, red Lego, red firetruck, red fish, red book, and red tractor in a basket.

2. Allow your child to explore all of the different objects of the same color. Some examples of physical traits to investigate are shape, smell, texture, weight, etc.

3. You can repeat this activity with other colors too. If you want to challenge your toddler, place objects of the same color in the basket and one object of a differing color in the same basket. Ask him to pick out the object that is a different color from the rest.

☆ Color on Sandpaper

S **C** **F** **Developmental Objective:** As your child colors, he will strengthen his fingers as he grasps crayons.

Materials:

☐ Sandpaper
☐ Crayons
☐ Painter's Tape

Directions:

1. Place a piece of sandpaper on the table. Use painter's tape to attach the sandpaper to the table to prevent the sandpaper from sliding around as your toddler colors.

2. Set your toddler at the table in front of the sandpaper and crayons.

    Quick Tip: I recommend using the fat crayons for children of this age because they are easier to grip.

3. Ask him to feel the sandpaper. Explain how the sandpaper is rough and the table is smooth. Have him feel the difference as you describe the two objects.

4. Now ask him to pick a crayon and begin drawing on the sandpaper.

5. When your child is finished with his masterpiece, talk to him about the colors he used and pictures he drew.

Colored Craft Stick Puzzle

S F **Developmental Objective:** Your child will develop his visual sense as he learns to identify matching colors.

Materials:

- ☐ Large Piece of White Paper
- ☐ Colored Craft Sticks
- ☐ Markers

Directions:

1. To prepare this activity, place the colored craft sticks on the piece of white paper in no particular order.

2. Trace around each craft stick's outline in the same color marker as the craft stick.

3. Remove the craft sticks from the paper and set to the side.

4. Ask your child to come do a puzzle with you. Show him how to match a colored craft stick to a matching colored spot on the paper.

5. Cheer him on as he completes the puzzle.

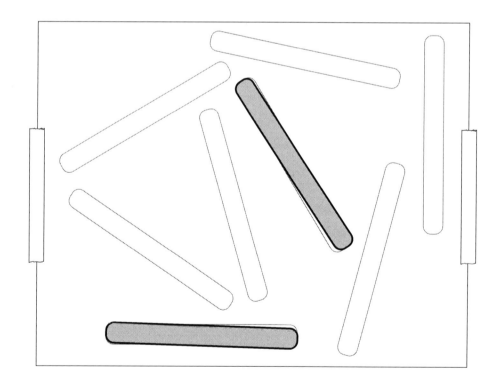

☆ Cushion Mountain

 Developmental Objective: This activity allows your child to enhance his sense of balance as he climbs over pillows and cushions.

Materials:

☐ Assortment of Cushions and Pillows
☐ Large Blanket
☐ Favorite Toy

Directions:

1. Gather a bunch of cushions and pillows from around your house.

2. Ask your toddler to help you stack the cushions and pillows into a mountain formation on the floor.

3. Spread a blanket over the top of the cushion mountain.

4. Place your child's favorite toy on the top of the cushion mountain.

5. Ask him to climb up the mountain to retrieve the toy and climb back down.

6. Do this as many times as he would like.

• • • • • • • • • • • •

☆ Cut a Banana

 Developmental Objective: Your child will develop his hand strength as he holds a plastic knife to cut a banana. He will also use his sense of smell and taste for this activity.

Materials:

☐ Peeled Banana
☐ Plastic Knife or Craft Stick
☐ Plate

Quick Tip: *I recommend teaching your child about knife safety even though he will be using a plastic knife.*

Directions:

1. Place a peeled banana on a plate.

2. Show your child how to hold a knife in one hand (if you are not comfortable with your child using a plastic knife, he may use a craft stick in its place) and banana in the other hand so that he can cut the banana.

3. Ask him to slice the banana.

4. Allow him to practice this new skill.

5. This is a fun activity for your toddler to do alongside you while you are cooking so that he is a part of the cooking experience too.

☆ Dot Sticker Tracing

> **S** **F** **Developmental Objective:** Your toddler will gain finger control as he removes stickers from the paper to place on a designated shape. He will also be able to use the sense of touch to feel the stickiness of the stickers.

Materials:

- ☐ 3 Pieces of Paper
- ☐ Marker
- ☐ Dot Label Stickers

Directions:

1. On one piece of paper use a marker to draw a large square. On the second piece of paper draw a large circle. On the third piece of paper draw a large triangle.

2. Place each shape in front of your toddler. Point to one shape and state the shape's name. Ask him to say the shape's name back to you. He can trace the outline of the shape with his finger.

3. Ask him to peel the dot stickers off the sheet of stickers and place them along the outline of the shape.

4. Repeat Steps 2 and 3 for the other two shapes. (If he doesn't put the stickers on the line don't worry, you can simply direct him where to place the stickers by pointing to the line of the shape.)

• • • • • • • • • • • • •

Drive Cars on Lines

> **F** **O** **Developmental Objective:** This outdoor activity will allow your child to develop his hand muscles and coordination as he holds a toy car in his hand to drive it on a single line.

Materials:

- ☐ Chalk
- ☐ Toy Cars

Quick Tip: This is a fun activity to do outside, but if weather conditions do not allow you can substitute chalk for painter's tape and do the activity inside.

Directions:

1. Using chalk, draw several 6-foot lines on the sidewalk. You can draw a straight line, wavy line, and zigzag line.

2. Now ask your child to pick a toy car.

3. He can pretend each line is a road and drive his car on each road. It's always fun to race the cars on the roads too. Holding a toy car helps strengthen the muscles in his hands.

4. After following the lines for a few minutes, it may be fun to add even sillier roads, parking lots, restaurants, etc.

Drive Through Tunnels

F **Developmental Objective:** Your toddler will strengthen his hand muscles as he holds and maneuvers toy cars through tunnels.

I

Materials:

- ☐ Tape
- ☐ 5 Pieces of Paper
- ☐ Toy Cars

Directions:

1. Lay each piece of paper in front of you in landscape orientation.

2. Fold the left edge of each paper inward one inch. Now, unfold it.

3. Fold the right edge of each paper inward one inch. Now, unfold it.

4. Hold the outside folded edges and move them close together so the center raises up until you form a small tunnel like the picture below.

5. Use the tape to adhere the folded edges to the floor or a table.

6. Repeat steps to create four other tunnels.

7. Ask your toddler to drive his toy cars through the tunnels.

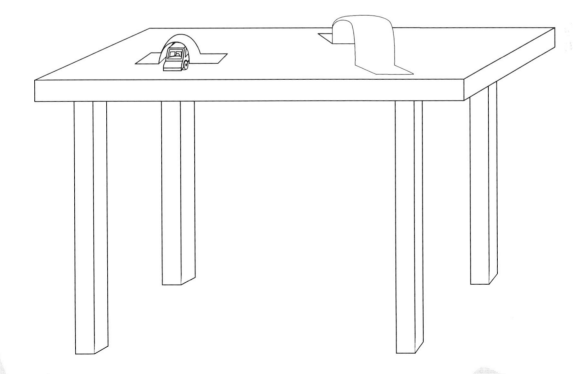

☆ Dry Noodle Sensory Bin

 Developmental Objective: This activity allows your toddler to play tactilely. He can use his hands to explore the texture of dry noodles.

Materials:

- ☐ Large Plastic Container
- ☐ Dry Pasta
- ☐ Small Toys

Directions:

1. Pour dried pasta into the large plastic container. This can be an assortment of pasta or just one type of pasta.

2. Bury small toys in the pasta to hide them.

3. Ask your toddler to dig through the pasta to find the hidden toys.

• • • • • • • • • • • • • • •

Edible Paint

S **C** **Developmental Objective:** This sensory activity allows your toddler to create a craft while enhances his sense of touch and taste.

Materials:

- ☐ Yogurt or Whipped Cream
- ☐ Food Coloring
- ☐ Muffin Tin

Directions:

1. Add a dollop of yogurt or whipped cream to four muffin tin cups.

2. Add 3-4 drops of red food coloring in the first muffin tin cup with the yogurt. Add blue food coloring to the second, green food coloring to the third, and yellow food coloring to the fourth.

3. Use a spoon to stir each edible paint mixture.

4. It is fun for your toddler to paint the table or his high chair tray using his fingers as a paintbrush. Paper is a good option too.

5. As he is painting, he can taste the paint.

Edible Sand

> **S** **O** **Developmental Objective:** This outdoor activity lets your child explore his sense of touch and taste while playing.

Materials:

- ☐ Graham Crackers
- ☐ Food Processor
- ☐ Large Plastic Container
- ☐ Sand Toys

Quick Tip: *This activity is best done outside.*

Directions:

1. To make edible sand, simply use a food processor or blender to chop the graham crackers into dust. You can choose how much graham cracker sand you would like to make.

2. When the sand is made, pour it into the large plastic container.

3. Add sand toys or other toys to the sand.

4. Invite your child to play in the sand. He can shovel the sand, make tracks in the sand with toy cars, or pour the sand over his fingers.

Envelope Flashcards

> **F** **Developmental Objective:** Your child will learn how to manipulate his fingers to open envelopes.

Materials:

- ☐ 10 Flashcards
- ☐ 10 Letter Envelopes

Quick Tip: *You may choose any type of child friendly flashcards to use (Ex. animals, colors, numbers, letters, etc.).*

Directions:

1. To prepare this activity, you will need to insert one flashcard into each envelope. Do not seal the envelope.

2. Ask your toddler to join you. Ask him to pick an envelope to open and find a surprise.

3. Allow him time to figure out how to open the envelope by himself and pull out the flashcard.

4. Talk about what is pictured on the flashcard.

5. Repeat until all envelopes are opened.

• • • • • • • • • • • • •

☆ Flashlight Exploration

> **S** **G** **Developmental Objective:** This activity encourages visual sensory play as your toddler explores the house with a flashlight. He will develop his gross motor skills as he maneuvers around furniture.

Materials:

- ☐ Flashlight

Safety Note: *Be sure to follow your toddler around the house closely so he does not get injured.*

Directions:

1. Turn off all lights in the house.

2. Give your toddler a flashlight and allow him to explore the house using a flashlight. It's a fun experience for your child to see the house in a different way, and it is exciting to use a flashlight!

Flower Sensory Bin

S O **Developmental Objective:** This outdoor activity allows your child to use his sense of touch and smell to investigate flowers.

Materials:

☐ Large Plastic Container
☐ Assortment of Flowers (Real or Fake)
☐ Water
☐ Cups, Bowls, Measuring Cups, etc.

Quick Tip: *If you choose to use real flowers for this activity, check the clearance section of your grocery store to save a few dollars. However, if you or your child has allergies, fake flowers are acceptable for this activity too.*

Directions:

1. Fill the large plastic container halfway with water and take outside.

2. Pull each stem off each flower. Place the flowers in the water.

3. Add cups, bowls, measuring cups, etc. to the water.

4. Invite your toddler to play in the flower bin. Ask him to smell the different flowers, feel the petals and the center of the flowers, or even break the flowers apart.

• • • • • • • • • • • • •

☆ Fort

G **Developmental Objective:** Your toddler will use his big muscle groups to manipulate pillows, cushions, and blankets as he builds a fort.

Materials:

☐ Cushions
☐ Pillows
☐ Blankets
☐ Chairs
☐ Box

Directions:

1. Use the above materials (or more) to create a fort with your toddler.

2. Play inside the fort together. You might even enjoy lunch together in the fort.

Free the Animals

 Developmental Objective: This sensory activity allows your toddler to build strength in his fingers as he opens Ziploc bags. This activity can be completed independently.

Materials:

☐ Small Toy Animals
☐ Sandwich Size Ziploc Bags

Directions:

1. Place one toy animal in a Ziploc bag, seal the bag. (If you do not have toy animals you can use toy cars, blocks, or even sliced fruit.)

2. Fill five Ziploc bags with toy animals.

3. Show your toddler the trapped animals. Explain to him that the animals need to be rescued from the bags. Tell him to open the bags and free the animals.

• • • • • • • • • • • • • • •

Frozen Paint

 Developmental Objective: This outdoor craft helps your toddler develop his visual senses as he paints with different colors.

Materials:

☐ Ice Cube Tray
☐ Washable Paint
☐ 6 Popsicle Sticks
☐ Paper (Optional)

Prep Note: *You will need to prepare for this activity the day before you want to do it.*

Directions:

1. To make frozen paint, squirt a dab of washable paint into each ice cube tray cup. Add water to each ice cube tray cup. Stir each mixture.

2. Break the popsicle sticks in half. Place one-half popsicle stick into each ice cube tray cup.

3. Place the ice cube tray in the freezer until the mixture is completely frozen.

4. Once frozen, remove the frozen paint from the ice cube tray. Place on a plate or pan and take outside.

5. Invite your child to hold the frozen paint by the popsicle stick and paint on paper or the sidewalk.

☆ Fruit Play

> **S** **O** **Developmental Objective:** This outdoor activity helps your child explore his sense of touch, smell, and taste as he explores the textures, smells, and tastes of different fruit.

Materials:
- ☐ Large Plastic Container
- ☐ Water
- ☐ Assortment of Fruit

Directions:
1. Fill the large plastic container half-full with water. Place an assortment of fruit in the container of water. You may choose to cut the fruit into pieces or leave it whole. You can use fruits such as: apples, oranges, pears, grapes, blueberries, mango, cantaloupe, or watermelon.

2. Allow your toddler to investigate the fruits and play with the fruits. Talk about the fruits' colors, textures, smells, and even taste the fruits together as he plays.

• • • • • • • • • • • •

Glitter Bottle

> **S** **Developmental Objective:** Your child's visual senses will be engaged as he watches the glitter move throughout the bottle.

Materials:
- ☐ Clear Plastic Bottle
- ☐ Mixing Bowl
- ☐ Funnel
- ☐ Fine Glitter
- ☐ Hot Water
- ☐ Whisk
- ☐ Food Coloring
- ☐ Clear Elmer's Glue

Prep Note: In case bottles in each home are a different size, I am going to use proportions for measuring the amounts of ingredients.

Directions:
1. Pour 20% Elmer's glue and 80% water into the mixing bowl. Add the desired amount of food coloring and glitter to the mixing bowl.

2. Whisk all ingredients together.

3. Pour the mixture into the plastic bottle right away so the glitter does not settle at the bottom of the mixing bowl.

4. Screw the lid tightly onto the plastic bottle. (If you have super glue then you can add a ring of super glue around the inside of the top before screwing it onto the bottle to prevent the bottle from opening.)

5. Allow your toddler to shake the bottle and watch as the glitter slowly begins to fall. This is a soothing experience.

☆ Glowstick Hide and Seek

(S) (G) _Developmental Objective:_ Your toddler will practice using his gross motor muscles and visual senses as he searches for hidden glowsticks.

Materials:

☐ 6 Glowsticks

Directions:

1. Crack six glowsticks so they begin to glow.

2. Explain to your child that you will hide the glowsticks around the room, turn off the lights, and then ask him to find the hidden glowsticks.

3. Ask your toddler to close his eyes. While his eyes are closed, hide the glowsticks in places where he can see the glow from the hidden location.

4. Turn off the lights.

5. Once the glowsticks are hidden, ask him to open his eyes and find the hidden glowsticks. Follow your toddler around as he is looking for the hidden glowsticks to help prevent any accidents.

6. After he finds all glowsticks, lay the glowsticks on the floor and practice pointing to and counting the glowsticks with your toddler.

7. Repeat this activity as many times as your child would enjoy.

• • • • • • • • • • • • •

☆ Go-Go-Go-Sit

(G) (O) _Developmental Objective:_ This outdoor activity allows your toddler to practice his coordination and balance as he runs around the yard.

Directions:

1. This is a fun activity to burn a lot of energy. You and your toddler will both run around the yard (or a room). You will continue to shout, "Go, go, go," as you both run.

2. When you get tired and need a break yell, "Sit." Both you and your child need to sit down right where you are immediately.

3. Count to ten out loud.

4. Then hop up and begin to shout, "Go, go, go," again as you and your child run.

5. Do this as many times as you need to until your little one is tired.

Golf Tee Hammering

F **G** **Developmental Objective:** Your toddler will strengthen his hand muscles as he holds a hammering. He will also strengthen his arm muscles and hand-eye coordination as he hits the golf tees with a hammer.

Materials:

- ☐ Cardboard Box
- ☐ Golf Tees
- ☐ Plastic Hammer

Directions:

1. Prepare this activity by using golf tees to poke holes into the cardboard box. You can poke holes in any pattern you choose, but if the box is large enough you could poke holes to form the letters of your child's name.

2. Keep the golf tees in each hole, but not pushed all the way down.

3. Hand your toddler the plastic hammer and allow him to hammer the golf tees down into the holes.

4. For a challenge, you can take the golf tees out of the holes and ask your toddler to place the golf tee in each hole and then hammer it.

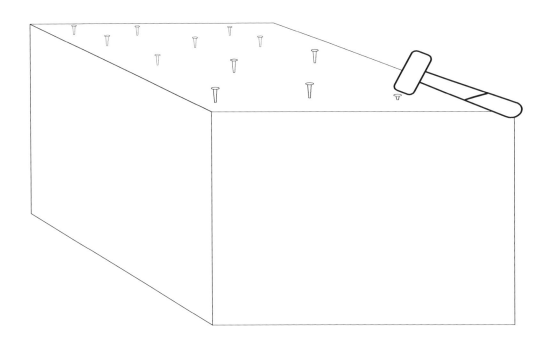

Grab the Spoon

> **F** **Developmental Objective:** This activity will develop your child's hand strength as he grasps each spoon.

Materials:

- ☐ Double-Sided Tape
- ☐ Plastic Spoons

Directions:

1. Pick a location that has an opening. For example, a bookshelf has an opening between each shelf. Place the double-sided tape from the ledge of one shelf to the ledge of the other shelf. This needs to be placed at a level your toddler can reach.

2. Stick the plastic spoons to the tape.

3. Invite your toddler over to the spoons. Ask him to remove each spoon from the tape. You can ask him to pull one spoon with his left hand and another spoon with his right hand for a challenge.

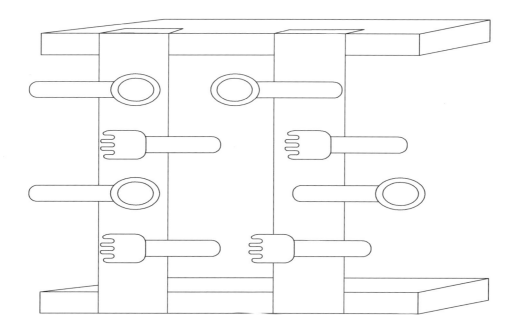

Grocery Store Scavenger Hunt

Developmental Objective: Your child will enhance his visual senses as he looks for each item on his shopping list.

Materials:

- ☐ Paper
- ☐ Grocery Store Ad
- ☐ Tape
- ☐ Marker
- ☐ Pencil

Directions:

1. Cut out five pictures from the grocery store ad of items that you will be purchasing on your trip to the grocery store.

2. Tape the pictures in the middle of the piece of paper like a list.

3. To the left of each picture, draw a square checkbox.

4. To the right of or under each picture, write the word of the item so that your toddler can begin to learn about letters and words.

5. When you arrive at the grocery store, hand your child the list you made. Ask him to identify each item on his list as you point to the pictures.

6. Explain to him that you will be buying the items, and you need his help finding the items on his grocery list. When he finds the pictured items on his list, he can put an "X" in the checkbox.

Hidden Puzzle Pieces

(S) (I) (F) **Developmental Objective:** This sensory activity allows your child to explore different textures as he finds wooden puzzle pieces in socks. As he holds each puzzle piece, he will build his hand strength.

Materials:

☐ Chunky Wooden Puzzle
☐ Socks

Quick Tip: *For this activity and for your child's age, puzzles with large wooden puzzle pieces are best.*

Directions:

1. Take each puzzle piece off the puzzle board. Place each puzzle piece inside its own sock.

2. Place the empty puzzle board in front of your toddler along with the socks filled with puzzle pieces.

3. Ask him to pick a sock, look inside the sock, reach inside the sock, and pull out the hidden puzzle piece.

4. He can then place the puzzle piece on the correct spot on the puzzle board.

5. Continue Steps 3 and 4 until the puzzle is complete. He may continue to do this activity with you or he can do it independently.

• • • • • • • • • • • • •

☆ Hide and Seek

(G) **Developmental Objective:** As your child maneuvers around the room to find a his animals, he will develop his gross motor abilities.

Directions:

1. At this age, your child likely will not fully grasp the concept of hide and seek, but he can still play variations of this classic kid's game.

2. Hide a few of his favorite stuffed animals, sit with him and count to 10 out loud.

3. Follow your child around and assist as needed to find all the animals.

4. Repeat as desired. If your child is ready, ask him to hide as you count.

5. Your child will likely need help if he is the "seeker" because counting is difficult. One option would be for you to hide and count out loud from another room, and then tell him when to find you.

☆ Ice Cube Water Bucket

 Developmental Objective: This outdoor activity allows your toddler to play tactilely. He can use his hands to explore the tempera-ture of the ice cubes.

Materials:

- ☐ Large Plastic Container
- ☐ Water
- ☐ Ice Cubes
- ☐ Food Coloring (Optional)
- ☐ Spoons, Bowls, Measuring Cups, etc.

Directions:

1. Outside, fill the large plastic container half-full with water.

2. Add food coloring and ice cubes to the water.

3. Allow your toddler to play in the water using spoons, bowls, measuring cups, etc. He can scoop the ice cubes out of the water into a bowl or play any way he chooses.

• • • • • • • • • • • • • •

I-Spy Bottle

 Developmental Objective: Your child's visual senses will be engaged as he investigates the items inside the bottle.

Materials:

- ☐ Empty Plastic Bottle with a Wide Mouth and Lid
- ☐ Rice
- ☐ Funnel
- ☐ Small Objects (Ex. Pom Poms, Plastic Animals, Foam Letters, Stars, etc.)

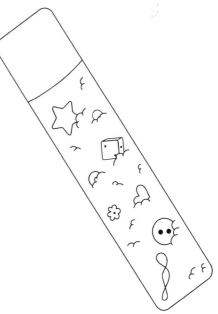

Directions:

1. In the empty bottle, insert the small objects you have collected.

2. Now, insert the funnel into the mouth of the bottle. Pour rice into the funnel—leave an inch of empty space at the top of the bottle.

3. Screw the cap onto the bottle.

4. Shake the bottle.

5. Hand the bottle to your child. Ask him what he sees inside the bottle as he shakes, spins, and looks at the bottle.

Jell-O Dig

> **S O** **Developmental Objective:** This outdoor activity allows your toddler to play tactilely. He can explore his sense of touch and taste as he plays.

Materials:
- [ ] Tupperware
- [ ] Jell-O Packet
- [ ] Water
- [ ] Spoons
- [ ] Small Washable Toys

Directions:

1. Using a Tupperware container, follow the directions on the Jell-O package to make Jell-O.

2. Before you place the Jell-O mixture in the refrigerator to firm, insert the small, washable toys inside the Jell-O.

3. Once the Jell-O is prepared, invite your toddler outside to dig through the Jell-O to rescue the toys. He may use spoons or his fingers.

• • • • • • • • • • • • •

☆ Junk Mail Basketball

> **G** **Developmental Objective:** Your child will gain hand-eye coordination as he practices his throwing skills.

Materials:
- [ ] Junk Mail
- [ ] Recyling Bin

Directions:

1. Ask your toddler to help crumble pieces of junk mail into balls.

2. Once you have the balls created, place an empty recycling bin in the center of the room.

3. Place your toddler three to six feet away from the recyling bin.

4. Ask him to throw the crumpled mail into the recyling bin.

5. Cheer him on as he makes a basket. You can hand him the missed shots so he can try again.

☆ Laundry Basket Fishing

> **F**
> **G** **Developmental Objective:** Your child will develop his fine motor skills as he grasps the tongs in his hand. He will as develop his spatial awareness as he reaches for each toy with the tongs.

Materials:

☐ Laudry Basket
☐ Tongs
☐ Bath Toys or Small Toys

Directions:

1. Place the laundry basket in the middle of the room.

2. Place your toddler inside the laundry basket. He can pretend it is a boat.

3. Place toys on the floor around the laundry basket (close enough for your child to reach).

4. Hand him the tongs. Ask him to go fishing for the toys by using the tongs to pick up the toys and place them inside the laundry basket with him.

• • • • • • • • • • • • •

☆ Learn Positions

> **G** **Developmental Objective:** This activity helps your toddler develop his gross motor strength as he bends, reaches, lifts, and squats to place his stuffed animal.

Materials:

☐ Favorite Stuffed Animal

Directions:

1. Grab your child's favorite stuffed animal. Hand it to your child.

2. Explain to him that you will call out a direction and he will need to place his favorite stuffed animal in that spot.

3. Feel free to call out the positions you would like, but here are some examples:

   a. Place your animal under the table.

   b. Place your animal behind the chair.

   c. Place your animal on top of the table.

   d. Place your animal beside the chair.

   e. Sit your animal on the chair.

Letter Fishing

Developmental Objective: This outdoor activity allows your child to play tactilely. He will begin to visually see the different letters of the alphabet.

Materials:

☐ Large Plastic Container
☐ Water
☐ Blue Food Coloring (Optional)
☐ Plastic or Wood Letters
☐ Mesh Strainer

Directions:

1. Outside, fill the large plastic container half-full with water.

2. Add blue food coloring to the water if desired.

3. Add the plastic letters to the water.

4. Hand the mesh strainer to your toddler. Ask him to use the strainer as a fishing net and fish out letters from the container.

5. As he fishes out the letters, you can lay them on the ground, point to them, and say the letter's name to him.

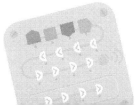

Lift the Flap Family

S **I** **F** ***Developmental Objective:*** Your toddler's senses will be engaged as he recognizes family member's pictures. He will practice using his fine motor skills to lift the flaps.

Materials:

- ☐ 2ft by 2ft Piece of Cardboard
- ☐ Printed Pictures of Family Members
- ☐ Plastic Wipe Lids that Open
- ☐ Tape
- ☐ Hot Glue Gun
- ☐ Scissors

Directions:

1. To make the "lift the flap" you will need to print a picture of each family member you would like to include in this activity. I recommend including a picture of your toddler too.

2. You will need to gather a plastic wipe lid for each picture you plan to include. (If you do not have the wipe lids, then you may cut out extra cardboard squares and tape them over the pictures as flaps.)

3. Place a wipe lid over each picture. Open the wipe lid to make sure when the lid is open the family member's face is seen. Then, cut the excess picture from around the outside edges of the wipe lid.

4. Tape each picture in place on the 2ft by 2ft piece of cardboard.

5. Hot glue the wipe lids on top of the pictures.

6. Present the lift the flap board to your toddler. Show him how to lift the lids to reveal the family member's picture.

7. Each time he lifts a lid, you can ask him to identify who is pictured.

☆ Match Socks

> **S**
> **G**
> **Developmental Objective:** This activity helps engage your toddler's visual senses and gross motor skills as he looks for and walks to matching socks.

Materials:
- ☐ Assortment of Socks

Directions:

1. Gather an assortment of socks from your home (you can choose to do this activity while you are folding laundry).

2. Lay the socks out around the floor.

3. Ask your toddler to pick up one sock.

4. Tell him there is another sock that looks exactly like the sock he is holding. Ask him to find the match and bring both to you.

5. Repeat Steps 3 and 4 until all socks are matched. This activity will allow him to feel like a helper.

• • • • • • • • • • • • • • •

☆ Match the Lid and Container

> **F**
> **I**
> **Developmental Objective:** This independent activity helps your child strengthen his fine motor skills as he manipulates the Tup-perware container lids to fit on the Tupperware.

Materials:
- ☐ Tupperware Containers
- ☐ Matching Tupperware Lids

Directions:

1. This is a great activity for your child to do while you are cooking dinner. Set out an assortment of Tupperware containers along with the matching lids. Include circle, square, and rectangle containers of varying sizes.

2. Separate the lids from the Tupperware container.

3. Now, ask your child to find the lid that will fit on each Tupperware container and place it on top.

4. Cheer him on as he finds the correct match.

☆ Memory Game

> **S** **Developmental Objective:** This sensory activity helps engage your child's visual, auditory, and recall skills as he sees, listens to, and remembers the picture on each card.

Materials:

☐ Flashcards

Quick Tip: *You may choose any type of child friendly flashcards to use (Ex. animals, colors, numbers, letters, etc.).*

Directions:

1. Lay four flashcards in front of your toddler.

2. Point to each card, name the pictured item on the card, and ask your child to name it too.

3. Flip the flashcards face down. Do not mix the flashcards.

4. Ask him to point to where one of the flashcard pictures is located. Turn it over to check if he is right. For example, if the flashcards that were face down were a dog, cat, fish and and bird, then you could ask your toddler to point to one of the four animals as they are face down. Then turn it over to see if he is correct.

5. If he got it right, he gets to keep the flashcard picture side up.

6. Continue to ask him to point to where the other pictures are located until all cards are face up.

Mix Colors in a Bag

 Developmental Objective: This color mixing activity enhances your child's visual senses by helping him recognize colors and make new colors.

Materials:

☐ 3 Gallon Size Ziploc Bags
☐ Red, Yellow, and Blue Washable Paint
☐ Tape

Directions:

1. Inside the first Ziploc bag, squirt a glob of red and blue paint on separate sides of the bag. Seal the bag.

2. Inside the second Ziploc bag, squirt a glob of red and yellow paint on separate sides of the bag. Seal the bag.

3. Inside the third Ziploc bag, squirt a glob of yellow and blue paint on separate sides of the bag. Seal the bag.

4. Place each bag on the floor or a table. Place tape across the seal and edges of the bag.

5. Invite your toddler to come investigate the bags. Ask him to identify the colors inside the first bag. If he is unfamiliar with the colors then you can tell him.

6. Ask him to mix the red and blue paint together to discover what new color is made in the process. Identify the color he has made as purple.

7. Repeat Steps 5 and 6 for the other two Ziploc bags. Red and yellow paint mixed together will make orange. Yellow and blue paint mixed together will make green.

Mud Sensory Bin

> **Developmental Objective:** This outdoor activity allows your toddler to play tactilely. He can use his hands to explore the texture of mud.

Materials:

- ☐ Large Plastic Container
- ☐ 1 Cup Cocoa Powder
- ☐ ½ Cup Cornstarch
- ☐ 1 Cup Water
- ☐ Toy Trucks

Directions:

1. In a large plastic container mix together cocoa powder, cornstarch, and water. You can double the recipe if you have a really big container.

2. Take the mud sensory bin outside.

3. Add toy trucks, animals, or rocks and invite your toddler to play in the mud. He can use his trucks to sort the rocks into piles of little and big in the mud sensory bin.

• • • • • • • • • • • • • •

Mystery Bag

> **Developmental Objective:** Your toddler will develop his sense of touch as he investigates mysterious objects in a bag.

Materials:

- ☐ Bag
- ☐ Objects from Around the House

Directions:

1. Gather a few familiar items and a few unfamiliar items from around the house (5-6 items are enough). Place the items in a bag.

2. Ask your toddler to place his hand inside the bag and feel the items.

3. Ask him to hold one of the items in his hand without pulling it out of the bag or looking inside the bag. Ask him questions about the item (is it soft, hard, prickly, round, etc.).

4. Then, let him pull the item out of the bag and identify it.

5. Repeat Steps 2-4 until the bag is empty.

☆ Nature Walk

S O G **Developmental Objective:** This outdoor activity helps your child develop his gross motor skills as he walks through nature.

Materials:

☐ Bucket with Handle

Directions:

1. Ask your toddler to go on a walk with you around the yard or neighborhood.

2. Hand him a bucket and tell him to find things in nature he thinks are neat to put in his bucket. He can find different color leaves, rocks, sticks, flowers, etc.

3. When you complete your walk, dump out the items in his bucket and explore them together. Count the items. Feel the different textures of the items.

4. Help sort the items into any interesting groups you can find (Ex. living/non-living, colors, heavy/lightweight, etc.).

• • • • • • • • • • • • • •

Obstacle Course

 Developmental Objective: Your toddler will strengthen his gross motor skills as he completes the obstacle course challenge by climbing, walking, running, kicking, pushing, or etc.

Directions:

1. Create an obstacle course for your child from the furniture around your home. Keep this simple for this age. Climbing, crawling, stepping over, ducking, hopping, etc. are all great ways to help build the big muscle groups in your child's body.

2. Here are some examples of things to include in the obstacle course:

    a. Climb over cushions

    b. Step over string

    c. Crawl through a blanket tunnel

    d. Slide down a slide

    e. Kick a soccer ball to the next obstacle

    f. Push a basket of toys to the next obstacle

☆ Paint on Foil

(S) (C) *Developmental Objective:* The sensory craft allows your child to explore his visual senses as he paints.

Materials:

- ☐ Aluminum Foil
- ☐ Tape
- ☐ Washable Paint
- ☐ Paper Plate
- ☐ Paintbrushes

Directions:

1. Lay a piece of aluminum foil on the table.

2. Tape it in place to prevent the aluminum foil from moving.

3. Squirt a few dollops of washable paint onto the paper plate.

4. Hand your toddler a paintbrush and ask him to paint a picture on the aluminum foil.

• • • • • • • • • • • • • •

☆ Paint on Ice Cubes

(S) (C) (O) *Developmental Objective:* This outdoor craft allows your child to develop his spatial awareness as he paints on the sliding ice cubes.

Materials:

- ☐ Ice Cubes
- ☐ Plate or Dish with Edges
- ☐ Washable Paint
- ☐ Paper Plate
- ☐ Paintbrushes

Directions:

1. Place a couple ice cubes onto a plate or dish with edges.

2. Squirt a dollop of washable paint onto the paper plate. You may choose a few colors

3. Hand your toddler a paintbrush.

4. Ask him to dip his paintbrush into the paint and paint the ice cubes. The ice cubes will slide around the plate, but that makes it more fun and challenging for little one.

Paint Sample Puzzles

S **F** **Developmental Objective:** Your child will use his visual senses to match the same colored pieces together. He will develop his fine motor skills as he uses his fingers to pick up the puzzle pieces.

Materials:

☐ Paint Sample Cards
☐ Scissors

Directions:

1. Grab some paint sample cards from your home improvement store the next time you go. Select five different colors.

2. Cut easy designs across each paint sample to cut them in half. Cut a different design into each of the five paint samples. For example, cut a zigzag pattern from one edge of the red paint sample to the opposite edge of the red paint sample.

3. Place all puzzle pieces in front of your child.

4. Ask him to find the matching pieces and fit them together to complete the puzzle.

5. This is an activity he might be able to do independently after he has done it with you.

• • • • • • • • • • • • •

☆ Paint with Water

S **O** **F** **C** **Developmental Objective:** This outdoor sensory craft allows your child to play tactilely with water. He will gain strength in his hand as he practices holding a paintbrush.

Materials:

☐ Cup
☐ Water
☐ Paintbrushes

Directions:

1. Fill a cup with water.

2. Ask your toddler to join you outside.

3. Show him how to dip his paintbrush in the water and paint a picture on the sidewalk.

4. You can use chalk to draw a picture on the sidewalk, and then your toddler can trace the chalk picture with his paintbrush and water.

☆ Pasta in Colander

F **Developmental Objective:** Your toddler will develop his pincer grasp as he picks up each spaghetti noodle with his index finger and thumb.

Materials:

☐ Colander
☐ Dried Spaghetti Noodles

Directions:

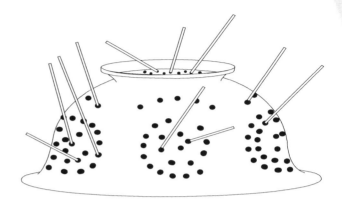

1. Turn a colander upside down.

2. Lay some dried spaghetti noodles beside your toddler and the colander.

3. Ask your toddler to pick up a spaghetti noodle and thread it through a hole in the colander.

4. He can continue to do this until all holes are full.

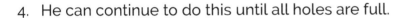

☆ Pea Smash

S **F** **Developmental Objective:** This sensory activity helps strengthen your child's fine motor skills as he smashes the peas with his fingers.

Materials:

☐ Quart Size Ziploc Bag
☐ Tape
☐ Peas

Quick Tip: *If the peas are frozen, please thaw them by heating them in the microwave. The time it takes to thaw the peas will depend on the amount of peas you choose to use.*

Directions:

1. Place the thawed peas in the Ziploc bag. Seal the bag.

2. Lay the Ziploc bag on the table or floor.

3. Use tape to adhere the edges of the bag to the table or floor.

4. Invite your toddler to use his fingers (or toes if the bag is on the floor) to smash the peas inside the bag.

Peekaboo Board

> **Developmental Objective:** Your toddler will be able to investigate new textures as he plays.

Materials:

- ☐ Muffin Tin
- ☐ Textured Items (Ex. Sandpaper, Cotton Balls, Slime, Orange Peel, Rock, etc.)
- ☐ Post-It Notes

Directions:

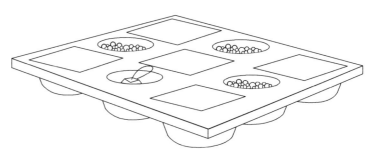

1. To prepare this activity, place one textured object inside each muffin tin cup. For example, place a rock in one muffin tin cup, place cotton balls in another muffin tin cup, place an orange peel in the third, and so on. Place a different item in each muffin tin cup until each cup has an item.

2. Now, place a Post-It Note over each muffin tin cup to cover the items.

3. Ask your toddler to come investigate the peekaboo board you have created.

4. Ask him to lift the Post-It Note off any one of the muffin tin cups. Ask him to feel the item inside.

5. Allow him to investigate the items inside each muffin tin cup. While he is feeling the item in each cup ask him questions about the way the item feels so he can learn new vocabulary about textures.

☆ Playdough Imprints

> **S** **Developmental Objective:** This activity allows your child to explore the texture of playdough and the effects of cutting, molding, and squishing playdough.

Materials:

- ☐ Playdough
- ☐ Cookie Cutters or Toys

Directions:

1. Invite your toddler to play playdough with you.

2. Flatten the playdough onto a flat surface.

3. Ask your toddler to press a cookie cutter or a toy into the playdough and pull it back out.

4. Let him see the imprint that is made from the cookie cutter or toy. He can then squish the shape in order to make a new one.

5. Play as long as he would enjoy.

• • • • • • • • • • • • • • •

Pom Pom Whisk

> **S** **I** **F** **Developmental Objective:** This sensory activity can help build your child's fine motor skills as he uses his index finger and thumb to grab pom poms. This activity can be completed independently.

Materials:

- ☐ Whisk
- ☐ Pom Poms
- ☐ Bowl

Directions:

1. Insert pom poms inside a whisk until no more pom poms will fit.

2. To keep your toddler busy, ask him to use his fingers to pull out each pom pom and place it in a bowl. Ask him to empty the whisk of pom poms.

Pom Pom Push

S **I** **F** **Developmental Objective:** Your toddler will gain control of his fingers as he uses them to push a pom pom through a hole. This activity can be completed independently.

Materials:

- ☐ Empty Oatmeal Container
- ☐ Scissors
- ☐ Marker
- ☐ Pom Poms

Directions:

1. You will need to cut holes into the oatmeal container lid, so use a marker to draw dime size circles on the lid of the oatmeal container. Draw three or four circles on the lid.

2. Use scissors to cut the circles out of the oatmeal lid.

3. Place the lid back onto the oatmeal container.

4. Place the oatmeal container in front of your toddler with a handful of pom poms.

5. Place a pom pom on top of the cut-out circle on the lid. Use one finger to push the pom pom through the hole.

6. Ask your toddler if he can push the pom poms into the holes.

☆ Post-It Note Books

S **F** *Developmental Objective:* Your toddler will engage his visual senses as he reads a book with you. He will build his fine motor skills as he pulls each Post-It Note off the page.

Materials:

☐ Children's Books
☐ Post-It Notes

Directions:

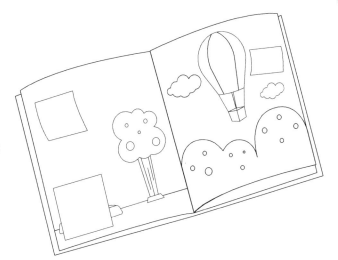

1. If your child is like my children, then he enjoys reading the same books again and again. You can spice up reading time by covering pictures in your child's favorite books with Post-It Notes prior to reading the book together.

2. As you are reading your child's favorite book ask him to pull the Post-It Note off the hidden picture to reveal what is underneath.

3. You can place the Post-It Note back in the book or leave it off the picture.

• • • • • • • • • • • • •

☆ Post-It Note Pull

F **G** *Developmental Objective:* This activity allows your child to develop his fine motor skills as he pulls the Post-It Notes off the wall and his gross motor skills as he reaches, bends, walks, etc. to reach the Post-It Notes.

Materials:

☐ Post-It Notes

Directions:

1. Stick Post-It Notes all over one room of your home. Stick them at varying heights so your child has to reach and squat to retrieve them. This is a great way to work on the gross muscles in his body.

2. After you have placed Post-It Notes everywhere, ask your toddler to find each one and pull it off. He can hand the Post-It Notes to you as he pulls them off or he can collect them in a bucket.

Pour Water

Developmental Objective: This outdoor sensory activity allows your toddler to gain coordination of his gross motor skills as he concentrates on pouring water into a cup.

Materials:

- ☐ Pitcher
- ☐ Water
- ☐ Cup

Directions:

1. Fill a pitcher with water to a level that is not too heavy for your toddler to lift.

2. Take the pitcher of water and a cup outside, along with your toddler.

3. Ask him to carefully pour the water into the cup. Explain he needs to be careful to not spill the water. (The water will certainly spill, and that's ok, but by telling him to try not to spill the water he will concentrate more on controlling the muscles he is using to pour the water.)

4. You can refill the pitcher so he can practice pouring water into the cup as many times as he would like.

5. After a few turns, it may also be fun to grab extra toys and play "restaurant" or "tea party."

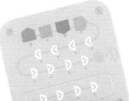

Push and Pull

S **Developmental Objective:** Your child will gain knowledge about different textures and colors as he completes this activity independently.

Materials:

- ☐ Piece of Cardboard
- ☐ Scissors
- ☐ Assortment of Ribbons

Directions:

1. Gather a piece of cardboard. It can be any size, but should be at least 8.5 inches x 11 inches.

2. Carefully, use scissors to poke holes into the cardboard in no particular order.

3. Cut different colored and textured ribbons at varying lengths.

4. Thread a ribbon through each hole in the cardboard.

5. Tie a knot into the ends of each ribbon so the ribbon does not slide out of the holes.

6. Hand your toddler the cardboard with ribbons. Ask him to pull one ribbon. As he is pulling, he can look on the back of the cardboard to see that the ribbon is getting shorter on the back side as it gets longer on the front. This is a fun way to begin to understand cause and effect.

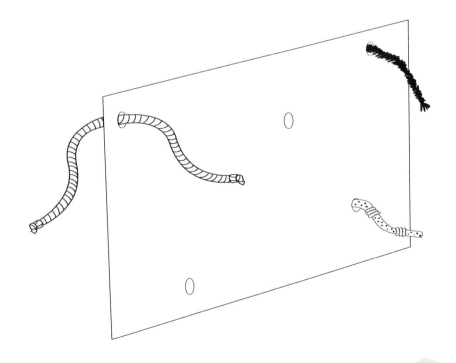

☆ Q-Tip Drop

> **F** **Developmental Objective:** This activity allows your toddler to refine his fine motor skills as he picks up Q-tips and places them into the jar.

Materials:

☐ Empty Grated Parmesan Cheese Container
☐ Q-Tips

Directions:

1. Place the empty container in front of your child along with a handful of Q-tips.

2. Open the side of the lid with the circle openings.

3. Show your toddler how one Q-tip can fit through the circle holes in the lid.

4. Ask him to pick up a Q-tip and slide it into a hole.

5. He can continue until his jar is full.

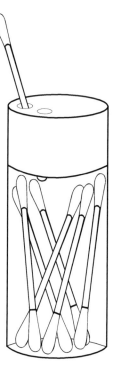

Rainbow Spaghetti

Developmental Objective: This outdoor activity allows your child to engage his visual and tactile senses as he plays with the spaghetti.

Materials:

- ☐ Spaghetti Noodles
- ☐ ½ Cup Vegetable Oil
- ☐ Bowls
- ☐ Food Coloring
- ☐ Pot
- ☐ Large Tupperware

Directions:

1. Cook spaghetti noodles according to the directions on the package.

2. Once cooked, drain the water and let the noodles cool.

3. Pour ½ cup of vegetable oil onto the noodles and mix well.

4. Now, you will need to divide the noodles evenly into separate bowls. You will need one bowl for each color you want to use.

5. In each bowl, add 10-12 drops of the desired food coloring. Mix well.

6. Pour all colored noodles into the large Tupperware.

7. Take the noodles and your toddler outside to play in the noodles. He can taste them, squish them in his fingers, or even stomp on them.

Ring Toss

 Developmental Objective: Your toddler will develop his gross motor skills coordination as he attempts to toss a ring.

Materials:

☐ 5 Pipecleaners
☐ Bucket

Directions:

1. Bring one pipecleaner's ends together to form a ring. Twist the ends together so that the ring does not come apart.

2. Create rings with all five pipecleaners.

3. Ask your toddler to join you. Hand him all five rings.

4. Place a bucket three to six feet from your toddler.

5. Ask your toddler to throw one ring at a time into the bucket. You might need to show him how to flick his wrist to toss the ring.

Sensory Walk

Developmental Objective: This activity allows your child to explore new textures and practice balancing as he walks across the sensory cards.

Materials:

☐ Cardstock
☐ Glue
☐ Sensory Items (Ex. Rice, Bottle Caps, Cotton Balls, Sponges, Yarn, Aluminum Foil, etc.)

Directions:

1. Decide how many sensory cards you would like to make. Pick one sensory item to go on each piece of cardstock. For example, you might choose to make a double-sided tape sensory card, a rice sensory card, a cotton ball sensory card, a sponge sensory card, and a bottle cap sensory card.

2. On each piece of cardstock, spread glue.

3. Stick the desired sensory item onto the glue.

4. Let dry.

5. Tape the sensory cards onto the floor.

6. Ask your toddler to walk to a sensory card and stand on it. Ask him how it feels under his feet. Ask him if he likes it.

7. Repeat Step 6 until all sensory cards have been tested.

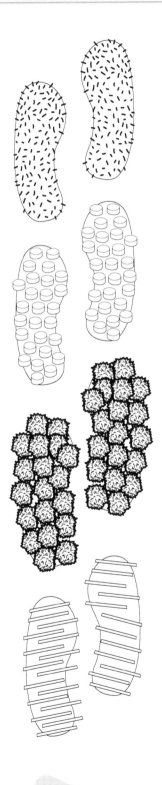

☆ Shake Painting

S O G C **Developmental Objective:** This outdoor craft helps strengthen your child's gross motor skills as he shakes the box. His auditory senses will also be engaged as he listens to the shaking box.

Materials:

- ☐ Shoebox
- ☐ Piece of Paper
- ☐ Tape
- ☐ Washable Paint
- ☐ Acorns, Rocks, or Marbles

Directions:

1. Take your toddler outside and ask him to collect acorns and/or rocks. If you do not have either of these items in your yard then you can use marbles.

2. Insert a piece of paper into a shoebox. Tape the corners of the paper down inside the box.

3. Ask your toddler to help you squirt a dab of washable paint onto the paper in the shoebox. You can choose to do one color or multiple colors.

4. He can now place the acorns or rocks inside the shoebox.

5. Close the lid of the shoebox.

6. Ask your toddler to place one hand on the lid and one hand on the bottom of the shoebox. Allow him to shake the box as hard as he can.

7. Open the lid to reveal the art he has created.

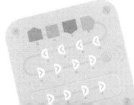

Shaker Balloons

(S) (G) Developmental Objective: Your child will enhance his auditory senses as he compares different sounds of each balloon. He will engage his gross motor skills as he shakes each balloon.

Materials:

- ☐ 6 Deflated Balloons
- ☐ Funnel
- ☐ 6 Items that Fit Through a Funnel (Ex. Oats, Sprinkles, Water, Rice, Beans, Beads, etc.)

Directions:

1. Insert a funnel into one deflated balloon.

2. Pour one of the six items (Ex. sprinkles) through the funnel into the deflated balloon.

3. Remove the funnel.

4. Blow the balloon up.

5. Tie the balloon off.

6. Repeat Steps 1-5 until all six balloons are inflated.

7. Ask your toddler to join you as you shake the balloons. Listen to the different sounds each balloon makes as it is shaken. You can determine which balloon is the quietest and which balloon is the loudest when shaken.

Shape Hunt in Rice

> **S O** **Developmental Objective:** This outdoor activity will allow your child to develop his visual and tactile senses as he compares the different shapes he finds in rice.

Materials:

- ☐ Large Plastic Container
- ☐ 5lb bag of Rice
- ☐ Wooden Shape Puzzle Pieces

Quick Tip: *If you do not have wooden shape puzzle pieces, then you can find objects around your home of each shape, or print out shapes from the computer and cut them out.*

Directions

1. Create a rice sensory bin by pouring a 5lb bag of rice into a large plastic container.

2. Insert and bury the wooden shape puzzle pieces.

3. Explain to your child that shapes are hidden in the rice and he must go on a treasure hunt to find the hidden shapes.

4. As he digs up each shape talk about the shape's name and how many sides it has. Ask him to repeat the shape's name to you.

5. Keep the rice sensory bin for repeated play sessions. It can be a fun place to push trucks, play with little figurines or just "make" food by pour ricing into other bowls or cups.

Shape Parking

S **F** **Developmental Objective:** Your child will engage his visual senses and fine motor skills as he picks up a toy car and identifies a shape.

Materials:

☐ Foam Shape Stickers
☐ Toy Cars
☐ Post-It Notes
☐ Painter's Tape

Directions:

1. You will need two of each kind of shape of the foam shape stickers, preferably the same colors too (Ex. 2 circles, 2 squares, 2 stars, etc.). Split the piles in half so that one of each shape is in each pile.

2. Gather the same number of toy cars as the number of shapes in one pile. So, if you have a circle, square, and triangle shape in one pile then you need three cars.

3. Using one of your foam shape sticker piles, place one shape sticker on the top of each toy car.

4. To make the parking lot, you will need to lay one Post-It Note down on the floor for each shape you have in one pile. (Ex. If you have three shapes, you need three Post-It Notes.)

5. Place one shape sticker on each Post-It Note.

6. Place a piece of painter's tape in between each Post-It Note to form parking spaces.

7. Explain to your toddler that he will pick one car, look at the top of the car to see what shape is on it then drive it to the parking spot (Post-It Note) with the matching shape.

8. As he picks out the cars, ask him to identify the shape on top of the car. Congratulate him as he matches the shapes correctly.

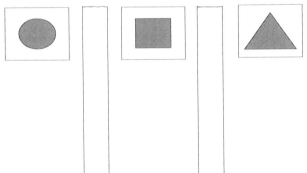

☆ Shaving Cream Colors

> **Developmental Objective:** This tactile activity will allow your child to strengthen his visual senses as he sees and identifies colors.

Materials:

- ☐ Tupperware
- ☐ Spoon
- ☐ Shaving Cream
- ☐ Food Coloring

Directions:

1. Place a Tupperware container in front of your toddler. Fill it with shaving cream.

2. Ask your toddler to pick two food coloring colors.

3. Squirt five drops of one food coloring on the left side of the shaving cream pile and five drops of the other food coloring on the right side of the shaving cream pile.

4. Hand him a spoon, and ask him to stir the shaving cream mixture to discover what happens.

5. You can do this experiment using different color combinations as many times as your child would enjoy.

Snack Math

> **Developmental Objective:** Your toddler will develop his fine motor skills as he picks up each snack item and places it on the circle. He will also engage his sense of taste as he snacks.

Materials:

☐ Paper
☐ Marker
☐ Snack (Ex. Goldfish Crackers, Grapes, Cheerios, etc.)

Directions:

1. Turn a piece of paper in landscape orientation.

2. Down the left side of the paper write the number "1" and draw one circle (the circle should be the size of the snack your child will enjoy) beside the number.

3. Under the "1," write the number "2" and draw two circles beside the number.

4. Under the "2," write the number "3" and draw three circles beside the number.

5. Under the "3," write the number "4" and draw four circles beside the number.

6. Under the "4," write the number "5" and draw five circles beside the number.

7. Ask your toddler to join you for snack time. Ask him to trace the number "1" with his finger and say, "one." Then he can place one of his snack items in the one circle.

8. Repeat Step 7 until all circles are filled in. Then he can enjoy his snack time.

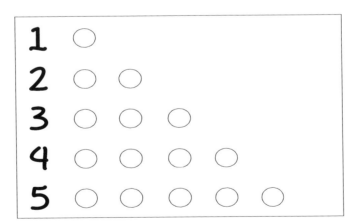

☆ Space Sensory Bin

> **S** **O** **Developmental Objective:** This outdoor activity allows your toddler to play tactilely. He can use his hands to explore the texture of the planets and stars.

Materials:

- ☐ Large Plastic Container
- ☐ Black Food Coloring
- ☐ Aluminum Foil
- ☐ Water
- ☐ Glow in the Dark Stars
- ☐ Scissors

Directions:

1. First, you will need to cut out a few circles from the aluminum foil—any size will do. These will be pretend planets for the sensory bin.

2. Fill the plastic container half-full with water. Take outside.

3. Add three drops of black food coloring. Mix well.

4. Add the glow in the dark stars and aluminum foil planets to the water.

5. Allow your toddler to play in the sensory bin as long as he would enjoy.

• • • • • • • • • • • • • •

Sponge Blocks

> **S** **I** **G** **Developmental Objective:** This independent activity reinforces your child's spatial awareness skills as he places blocks on top of each other. The sponge blocks provide your child with a new texture to explore.

Materials:

- ☐ 8 Rectangle Sponges
- ☐ Scissors

Directions:

1. Cut the eight sponges into varying sizes of rectangles and squares to resemble blocks.

2. Present your toddler with the sponge blocks.

3. Together with you or independently allow your toddler to build a tower out of the sponge blocks.

4. Keep blocks for the *Water & Sponge Sensory Bin* activity.

Squish Playdough

S **F** **Developmental Objective:** This sensory activity allows your toddler to strengthen his finger muscles as he squishes the playdough with each finger.

Materials:

☐ Playdough

Directions:

1. Pinch off a piece of playdough and roll it into a ball. Roll ten pieces of playdough into balls.

2. Line the balls of playdough up on the edge of a table or the floor.

3. Now, ask your toddler to use only one finger to squish each ball of playdough flat. You can ask him to use a new finger with each ball to help strengthen each finger or let him use a finger of his choosing for all balls of playdough. This will help build the muscles in his fingers that he will eventually need for writing.

4. Reset the activity and do it again if your child is interested.

• • • • • • • • • • • • • •

☆ Stack Cups

G **I** **Developmental Objective:** This independent activity will allow your child to develop his gross motor skills as he gathers cups from around the room and focuses on stacking them together.

Materials:

☐ Pack of Solo Cups

Directions:

1. Spread out the cups from the pack of Solo cups across the floor.

2. Demonstrate to your toddler how the cups can be stacked together.

3. Ask him to gather all the cups from around the room and stack them together.

4. Next, show him how to use the cups to build pyramids or various other towers.

5. Your child may also find it fun for you to build a tower and let him knock it down.

☆ Sticky Wall

> **S** **I**
> **C**
> **Developmental Objective:** Your toddler will create a craft as he uses his sense of touch to feel the texture of each craft item he places on the contact paper. This activity can be done independently.

Materials:

- ☐ Clear Contact Paper
- ☐ Tape
- ☐ Craft Supplies (Ex. Googly Eyes, Pom Poms, Pipecleaners, Beads, etc.)

Directions:

1. Cut out a piece of contact paper, 13 inches by 13 inches, or any size you prefer.

2. Lay the contact paper flat on a table, sticky side up.

3. Remove the protective film so the contact paper is now sticky.

4. Tape the edges of the contact paper onto the table so the contact paper stays in place.

5. You can lay out craft supplies (if you do not have craft supplies, feel free to use objects from nature), and invite your child to come create a masterpiece by sticking the items to the contact paper.

6. Talk about what he created once he finishes his work.

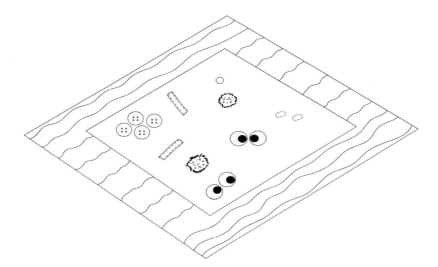

☆ String Cereal

> **F** **Developmental Objective:** Your child will reinforce his fine motor skills as he grabs each piece of cereal and threads it onto the pipecleaner.

Materials:

- ☐ Pipecleaner
- ☐ Cheerios or similar "O shaped" snack
- ☐ Playdough

Directions:

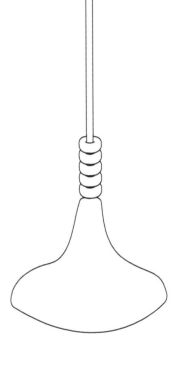

1. Make a big ball of playdough.

2. Stick a pipecleaner in the center of the playdough with only one end of the pipecleaner showing.

3. Now, stick the ball of playdough to a flat surface. The playdough is the anchor for the pipecleaner—it will help hold the pipecleaner in place.

4. Ask your toddler to join you. Give him a small bowl of Cheerios.

5. Ask him to thread one Cheerio at a time onto the pipecleaner. This is a great way to practice using the thumb and index finger (the same fingers needed to hold a pencil).

6. He can continue threading Cheerios until the pipecleaner is full.

☆ Sweep Pom Poms

F **G** **Developmental Objective:** This activity allows your toddler to develop his fine motor skills as he holds the hand broom. He is also building his gross motor skills as he completes the sweeping motion.

Materials:

- ☐ Painter's Tape
- ☐ Hand Broom
- ☐ Pom Poms

Directions:

1. Using painter's tape, tape out a square on the floor. You want the square to be at least 2 feet by 2 feet.

2. Place a bunch of pom poms on the floor outside the taped square.

3. Hand your toddler the hand broom. Ask him to use the broom to sweep all the pom poms into the square.

4. You can reset the game after he completes the task.

☆ Teddy Bear Play

> **G** **Developmental Objective:** Your toddler will build his gross motor skills as he makes big movements to place the teddy bear in the right location.

Materials:
- ☐ Favorite Stuffed Animal

Directions:

1. Ask your child to get his favorite stuffed animal. You can also grab a stuffed animal for yourself.

2. You will call out directions and your child will need to complete the movement using his teddy bear. You can use your stuffed animal to complete the directions as an example. Here are the movements:

      a.   Throw your teddy bear up and catch it.

      b.   Put your teddy bear on your head and walk around the room.

      c.   Spin around with your teddy bear.

      d.   Jump with your teddy bear.

      e.   Put your teddy bear on your shoulder.

      f.   Put your teddy bear on your elbow.

      g.   Put your teddy bear on your knee.

      h.   Put your teddy bear on your back.

      i.   Put your teddy bear on your stomach.

      j.   Put your teddy bear on your toes.

      k.   Put your teddy bear on your arm.

Tissue Box Surprise

S **I** **F**   ***Developmental Objective:*** This independent activity allows your child to build his fine motor skills as he uses his fingers to grab toys out of the tissue box. He is also using his sense of touch.

Materials:

☐ Empty Tissue Box
☐ Toys or Objects from Around the House

Directions:

1. When you have an empty tissue box you can use it for this activity. Gather a few small objects from around the house that will fit inside the tissue box.

2. Place the objects inside the box.

3. Hand the tissue box to your toddler.

4. Ask him to reach inside the tissue box and pull out an object. Talk about the object he pulled out—name it, talk about the texture, talk about the object's size, etc.

5. Continue Step 4 until all objects are out of the box.

6. You can refill the box with new items each time you want to do this activity with your child.

• • • • • • • • • • • • •

Trapped Toys

F **G**   ***Developmental Objective:*** Your toddler will strengthen his hand-eye coordination as he maneuvers his hand through the rubber bands. He will also develop his fine motor skills as he grabs the toys inside the pan.

Materials:

☐ Bread Pan
☐ Small Toys (Ex. Toy Cars, Ball, Plastic Animals, etc.)
☐ 6-10 Rubber Bands

Directions:

1. Gather a few small toys and place them inside a bread pan.

2. Carefully slide rubber bands around the top and bottom of the bread pan to trap the toys. Depending on the size of the bread pan, you will need 6-10 rubber bands spread evenly across the pan.

3. Place the trapped toys in front of your toddler. Ask him to free the toys by sticking his hand through the rubber bands and lifting the toys out of the pan.

Unwrapping Toys

(S) (F) Developmental Objective: This tactile activity allows your child to discover a new texture of aluminum foil. He will build his fine motor skills as he uses his fingers to unwrap each toy.

Materials:

☐ Aluminum Foil, Extra Newspaper or Similar for Wrapping
☐ Toys

Directions:

1. Gather a few of your child's toys that he has not seen or played with in a while.

2. Use sheets of aluminum foil to wrap the toys like a present. You can substitute aluminum foil for wrapping paper or tissue paper if you choose.

3. Place the wrapped toys in front of your toddler. Ask him to unwrap the toys. Feel free to add a creative story about how the toys were accidently wrapped up (Ex. the other toys wrapped these toys, the toy got stuck in the aluminum foil kitchen drawer, etc.).

4. Bonus, it will also get him excited about toys he has forgotten.

• • • • • • • • • • • • •

☆ Vegetable Play

(S) (O) Developmental Objective: This outdoor activity helps your child explore his sense of touch, smell, and taste as he explores the textures, smells, and tastes of different vegetables.

Materials:

☐ Large Plastic Container
☐ Water
☐ Assortment of Vegetables

Directions:

1. Fill the large plastic container half-full with water. Place an assortment of vegetables in the container of water. You may choose to cut the vegetables or leave them whole. You can use vegetables, such as: carrots, squash, okra, celery, corn, etc.

2. Allow your toddler to investigate the vegetables and play with the vegetables. Talk about the vegetables' colors, textures, smells, and tastes as he plays.

☆ Walk on Bubble Wrap

S **G** **Developmental Objective:** This sensory activity will develop your child's auditory skills as he listens to the bubble wrap, as well as his gross motor skills as he walks across the bubble wrap.

Materials:

- ☐ Long Piece of Bubble Wrap
- ☐ Tape

Directions:

1. Roll out a long piece of bubble wrap across the floor.

2. Tape the edges of the bubble wrap to the floor.

3. Hold your toddler's hand as he walks across the bubble wrap. He can choose to hold your hand and jump across the bubble wrap if he pleases.

• • • • • • • • • • • • • •

☆ Walk on Lines

G **O** **Developmental Objective:** This outdoor activity will help develop your child's balancing skills as he tries to stay on a single line.

Materials:

- ☐ Chalk

Directions:

1. Using chalk, draw a solid, straight line, a wavy line, a zigzag line, and a dashed line on the driveway or sidewalk.

2. Demonstrate to your toddler that he will walk on each line by placing one foot in front of the other as if he is walking on a tightrope. On the dashed line, he will need to jump at each break in the line.

3. Allow your toddler to try by himself.

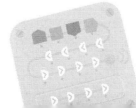

☆ Wash Toys

> **S** **O** **Developmental Objective:** This outdoor activity allows your toddler to play tactilely. He can use his hands to explore the texture of the toys, water, bubbles, and towel.

Materials:

- ☐ 2 Plastic Containers
- ☐ Water
- ☐ Toothbrush
- ☐ Towel
- ☐ Dish Soap
- ☐ Sponge
- ☐ Dirty Toys

Directions:

1. Fill both plastic containers half-full with water.

2. In one plastic container, squirt dish soap. Stir the soap around the container to form bubbles.

3. Ask your toddler to gather some dirty toys and take them outside to the containers of water.

4. Ask him to place the dirty toys in the soapy water.

5. Now, show him how to use the sponge and toothbrush to wipe the dirt off the toys.

6. Once he feels the toy is clean, ask him to rinse the soapy toy in the clean water to get the soap off of the toy.

7. Then he can use the towel to dry the toy off.

8. Continue Steps 5-7 until all toys are clean.

☆ Water and Sponge Sensory Bin

> **S** **O** ***Developmental Objective:*** This outdoor activity allows your toddler to play tactilely. He can use his hands to explore the texture of the water and sponges.

Materials:

- ☐ Large Plastic Container
- ☐ Water
- ☐ Sponges

Directions:

1. Fill the large plastic container half-full with water.

2. If you created sponge blocks from the *Sponge Blocks* activity you may use the same sponges for this activity. Regular sponges will work fine too. Place the sponges in the container of water.

3. Allow your toddler to play in the sensory bin as long as he would enjoy.

• • • • • • • • • • • • •

Water Bead Sensory Bin

> **S** **O** ***Developmental Objective:*** This outdoor activity allows your toddler to play tactilely. He can use his hands to explore the texture of the water beads.

Materials:

- ☐ Large Plastic Container
- ☐ Water
- ☐ Water Beads
- ☐ Bowl

Directions:

1. This activity will take an hour or more to prepare the water beads, but water beads are a fun experiment all on their own so let your little one help with preperation. He can see the beads go from tiny to big. Follow the directions on the water bead packaging to prepare the water beads.

2. Once the water beads are prepared, pour them into the large plastic container outside.

3. Allow your toddler to feel, squish, sit in, step on, and play with the water beads as long as he pleases.

A Gift for You

In appreciation of your purchase of this book, I would like to provide you with a link to enjoy 4 free activities your child is sure to enjoy. These activities are from *Toddler Lesson Plans: Learning Colors* and *The Ultimate Toddler Activity Guide*. Please follow the link below to access your free digital download.

www.bestmomideas.com/1-year-old-printouts
Password: bestmomideas26y8

Thank you for welcoming me into your home!
I hope you and your child liked learning together with this book!

If you enjoyed this book, it would mean so much to me
if you wrote a review so other moms can learn from your
experience.

-♡-
Autumn

Autumn@BestMomIdeas.com

Discover Autumn's Other Books

Early Learning Series

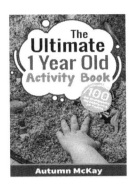

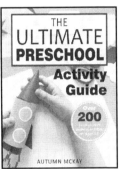

Early Learning Workbook Series

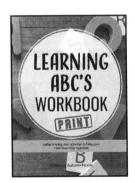

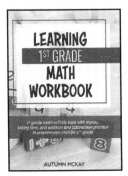

Made in the USA
Columbia, SC
01 May 2023

16000327R00048